I'm different, get over it!!

Nicola Wood

Presentation by *BookLeaf Publishing*

Web: www.bookleafpub.com

E-mail: info@bookleafpub.com

ISBN: 9789357442091

First edition 2023

*For all the people I know who face
challenges and difficulties on a daily basis
but still plod on with their life and achieve
so many amazing things.*

Acceptance

All
Courageous
Children
Enjoy
Performing
Together
At
Nice
Comfortable
Environments

At the park

Arriving at the park,
with my sister in tow.
Ready to watch,
her ability grow.

Sitting watching closely,
As she whisks on by.
Running, jumping, climbing
Tall to reach the sky.

Holding onto the ropes
As she steps one and two,
Getting higher and higher,
Higher than we ever knew.

Sitting on the bench,
soaking up the sun rays.
Sitting there all solemn,
thinking about my delays.

Why oh why, as a child
I couldn't do that
Oh well, I'm different,
I am me, and that's a fact.

Bereavement

Here I sit, so very still.
Curling up into a ball,
Looking up to the sky, until
I see that shooting star fall.

A smile enters my face,
A warmth powers over me
As the feeling of your body, I embrace
and the look into my eye, I see.

Your presence is here,
As I feel you close,
smelling your scent is clear.
There I sit on the windowsill, froze.

Good times fade,
but memories last.
The chances were made,
There in the past.

Times can be hard,
Without you by my side.
The heartache did leave me scarred.
But continuing life, I took in my stride.

Blossoming

At the start of its life,
A flower is a bud.
It sits there in the water,
And does as it should.

Soaking up the water,
It begins to rise.
The petals unfolding,
to reveal the disguise.

All the goodness and wealth
is now tied up inside.
Release from the plant pot,
and take life in your stride.

Enjoy the freedom,
The whole world around you.
Absorb the nature,
And the life you pursue.

Coming out

Hiding in a shadow,
A dark cloud over me.
The fear to show
an identity, that wasn't me.

Pretending to be
a girl people would adore,
but in deep reality,
a hatred grew inside.

These feelings I do face,
are not unusual.
My happiness I do embrace,
as this is my life.

Lesbian, Bi or Gay.
Pansexual, Trans or straight
Who has the right to say,
We are our own individual.

A world lifted of my shoulder,
when telling everyone.
But an almighty boulder
Came down with a thud.

Acceptance was slow
of my relationship status
which came as a blow
from my loved ones.

Disabilities

Different
Individuals
Struggle
Abit
But
In
Life
Individuals
Try
Identifying
Every
Strength

Hospital visits

Morning dawns, and birds tweet.
Everybody at the dining table
Surrounding that empty seat.
Noises escalate around.

Through the house and up the stair,
Noises fade and silence appears.
Each and everyone so unaware,
of the feelings of one girl.

With a creak of a door
And the switch of a light
There, a girl stood on the floor,
hand placed on the mirror.

Standing there, Staring back
Both thinking aloud.
Belly rumbling, ready for a snack
But no that's not for a while.

A journey in the car we go,
Windows up, music on
Just a girl and mum in tow,
On the busy road.

Parking up and nipping out,
Over the busy road, we go
Tummy now turning, with some doubt
About the hospital, we are now at.

Hospitals have been my place to stay
At times of need,
Just glad mum didn't stay away
On operating days.

I am me!

Brown hair or blonde
Long, short or spiky
Grey, white or ginger locks
Curly whirly, woo

I am me!

Long or little
Tall as a stick
Big or small
Short as a bean.

I am me!

Fast as a cheetah
Slow as a tortoise
Loud as a lion.
Quiet as a mouse.

I am me!

Inclusion

If
No-one
Can
Learn,
Understand,
Stick-by.
Isolation
Occurs
Naturally.

Inclusion is important.
Include individuals.

Individual

Everyone deserves a life
of acceptance and worth.
Everyone has the right,
for their demons to unearth.

Individually
No-one
Deserves
Intimidating
Violation
Interrupting
Days,
Unfortunately
Attacks
Lie

Labels

Labels, labels everywhere
On clothes and teabags
Rugs and carpets for your stair.
Labels, tags, and stickers too.

Labels are found in cafes and shops.
Expensive or cheap,
Wait till the price drops.
Then rip the tag off.

People are not defined,
By a condition, they may have.
Whether being deaf or being blind,
They are that person from within.

A person comes as a pack,
Their features and clothes, their individuality.
Not with a label stuck on their back.
A label is for displays in a shop.

Masking

Being in a crowded room,
People watch and stare.
Sitting there, when they assume,
You're just quiet in yourself.

Loud voices, the sound of chatter
Comes from all around.
Absorbing the enormous scatter,
Fuzzing of my brain goes.

Feelings of red, embrace on through.
The tension pulsates on down.
Too much to handle, wish they knew
This explosion that's about to erupt.

Now time to go,
Exhaustion has hit.
Tomorrow though,
Is a new day.

Meltdowns

Wind blowing through my hair,
Hands gliding over blades of grass.
Feelings of peace with not a care,
Staring over the peaceful land.

Sweeping under my nose
is the morning fresh air.
While birds compose
their harmonious tune.

Looking down, with nothing to spare
With a flash in my eyes
Chaos appeared everywhere.
A different world was seen.

A rumble, a roar
An explosion that burst
What is it, that my eyes saw,
But red.

Head is a fuzz
My hands are all sweaty,
Hearing is a buzz
AHHH….. what can I do.

With a shout and a scream,
That is all I can do.
Can I awake from this dream,
and just start again.

The taunt and upset
When this torture occurs.
The times that I fret
When my meltdowns arise.

Strong

Some people face the unknown.
Some people face challenges each day.
Some people face things, feeling alone.
Some people stand together and pray,
Some people are STRONG.

Think about others in hours of need,
Think about others when they are alone,
Think about others when their insides bleed.
Think about others in the times of the unknown.
Think about the times that you're STRONG.

Reflect on the times that we share,
Reflect on the moments of laughter and fun.
Reflect on the people who have been there,
Reflect on the love from that someone.
Reflect on the person you are, who's STRONG.

Of all the things we do,
Of all the stuff we say,
Of all the lessons we knew,
Of all the times we play.
Of all our life, we are STRONG.

Now is a pleasure,

Now is a time of hope,
Now is a treasure,
Now is how we cope.
Now is the time to be STRONG.

Great things happen in our life,
Great things blossom with our friends,
Great things are in our wildlife.
Great things do come to an end.
Great things occur when we are STRONG.

Triggers

To
Regularly
Independent
Gadgets
Grab
Eradicate
Responses
Seriously

Unique

Unlike university undergraduates,
Usually, Uncles Understand Uniqueness.
Unfortunately, undertakers usually undertake
using ugly uniforms.

Uniqueness is what we should be.
We should be loud and proud.
This poem as you can see,
Is Unique in its own right.

We are one

One person
One dog
One house
One car
One street
One shop
One village
One neighborhood
One community
One town
One city
One society
One country
One world

We are One

We shape a life

In a world of man and mouse.
We shape a life,
of adventures in every house.
Memories that we cherish forever.

The moulding of us all,
comes in shapes and sizes,
but as a whole,
We shape a life.

www.ingramcontent.com/pod-product-compliance
Lightning Source LLC
LaVergne TN
LVHW050301200726
843509LV00015B/3092